D1330935

To Jim,

We hope you'll come to see us in Wiltshire to show you around the beautiful countryside.

Cecile & Gwynne

WILTSHIRE

from the Air

WILTSHIRE
from the Air

JASON HAWKES

HALSGROVE

First published in Great Britain in 2010

Copyright © Jason Hawkes 2010

All rights reserved. No part of this publication may be reproduced,
stored in a retrieval system, or transmitted in any form or by any
means without the prior permission of the copyright holder.

British Library Cataloguing-in-Publication Data
A CIP record for this title is available from the British Library

ISBN 978 0 85704 004 6

HALSGROVE
Halsgrove House,
Ryelands Industrial Estate,
Bagley Road, Wellington, Somerset TA21 9PZ
Tel: 01823 653777   Fax: 01823 216796
email: sales@halsgrove.com

Part of the Halsgrove group of companies
Information on all Halsgrove titles is available at: www.halsgrove.com

Printed and bound by Grafiche Flaminia, Italy

INTRODUCTION

Wiltshire is a land of great antiquity. Its prehistoric monuments at Stonehenge, Avebury and Silbury Hill – some of the best in Europe – bear witness to the settlement of early man on its hills and downs. Wiltshire has developed as a largely agricultural landscape of farms and woods, but the great Salisbury Plain at its heart, the training ground of the British Army for generations, has remained a semi-wilderness, precisely because farming has been so restricted there.

Wiltshire's many attractive market towns and villages, built over the centuries from the profits of farming and its allied trades, especially wool, are dominated on the one hand by industrial and commercial Swindon (historically part of Wiltshire although today its own unitary authority) and on the other hand by historic Salisbury. Salisbury Cathedral's spire soars over the city, still medieval at its core, and seems to have been here from time immemorial. In fact, of course, Salisbury as we know it today is a "new" creation – the original town, Old Sarum, complete with cathedral, stood up on the hill above the present city, and was progressively abandoned after 1220 when the new settlement was established in the valley below.

The county's historic wealth is also reflected in the many mansions and landscape gardens for which it is famous. Longleat, Lacock Abbey, Bowood, Corsham Court, Wilton and Stourhead are all, for various reasons, among the most celebrated in the land. Wiltshire lay on the vital trade route between London and Bristol, for centuries the gateway to Atlantic commerce. The Kennet and Avon Canal provided an important waterborne link at the end of the eighteenth century until it was superseded by the Great Western Railway in the nineteenth century. Nearer to our own time, the construction of the M4, connecting London with South Wales and the West, has brought considerable prosperity to the motorway corridor in the north of the county.

All of these features, attractive or otherwise, become even more dramatic when seen from a "bird's eye" view. The fascinating aerial photographs in this book by internationally-renowned photographer Jason Hawkes are selected to provide the reader with an overview of this great variety of landscapes and settlements, with historic sites included. There can be no better way of appreciating the many glories of Wiltshire than to view the county from above.

The principal attraction of aerial photographs is that they allow us to look down on the landscape from a perspective that we never normally see. Such pictures reveal to us things that are normally hidden from view, and often surprise us when we find that what we had imagined the layout of the land to be is in reality quite different. The best practitioners of this genre of photography also strive to capture an aesthetic in the images they take, and these pictures, sometimes quite abstract in appearance, are often strikingly beautiful in their own right.

Savernake Forest. Today it is the only ancient forest still in private hands, although since 1939 it has been run by the Forestry Commission on a 999 year lease.

Above: Edington, about 5 miles east of Westbury. Perhaps its most distinguished feature is the Priory Church of St Mary, St Katherine and All Saints, which can be seen middle left.

Opposite: Dramatic fields of poppies have become more common in Wiltshire's arable land as the use of chemical sprays has diminished.

A typical chalk river scene near Salisbury. Salisbury sits at the confluence of five rivers, the Bourne, Ebble, Wylye and Nadder which are tributaries of the Avon.

Fovant Down Badges. The badges were cut in the chalk by soldiers garrisoned near Fovant in the Great War. In 1918 there were some twenty discernible badges in the area. There are only eight badges remaining although some have only recently been lost: the outline of the YMCA badge (second left) can just be seen.

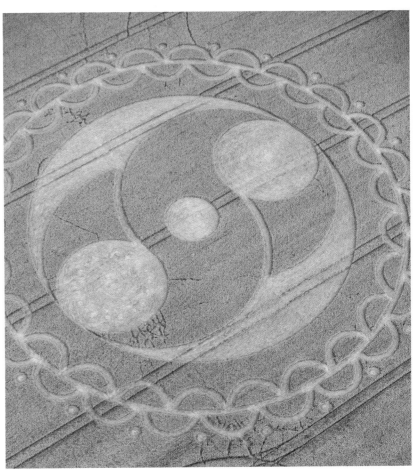

Above: Crop circle near Bishop Cannings.

Left: Crop circle near Barbury Castle, Overtown, Swindon. The crop circle phenomenon began in the 1970s and the presence of many near sacred sites in Wiltshire led to speculation that they were related to paranormal or extra-terrestrial activity. In fact, however, they are man-made works of art and despite their seeming complexity are often made with the simplest of tools.

A Chinook helicopter over Salisbury Plain. Roughly half of the Plain – some 150 square miles (390 sq km) – is owned by the Ministry of Defence and this is the largest military training area in the UK.

Tedworth House is owned by the MOD. It was formerly the seat of the Studd family, and was home to the three famous Victorian cricketing Studd brothers – Charles, Kynaston and George – who are referred to in the inscription on the Ashes urn.

A303 cutting through the Wiltshire countryside near Andover. The 303 is one of the main arterial routes between London and the South West. Although this section is dualled, substantial sections remain as single carriageway.

London Road and the A345 at Amesbury. Stonehenge lies in the parish and there is evidence of prehistoric settlement all around Amesbury. Although Pevsner describes Amesbury as "singularly devoid of houses of special interest" the town is a pleasing mix of old and more modern architecture.

Above: St Mary and St Melor Abbey Church, Amesbury. A Benedictine abbey was founded on the site of an earlier monastery by Dowager Queen Ælfthryth in 979. This became a priory of the Fontevrault order in 1177 and subsequently the parish church.

Right: Salisbury Street and Church Street, Amesbury.

Above: Newly-built estate of housing on the edge of Amesbury.

Left: Amesbury expanded considerably following the creation of the Aeroplane Armament Experimental Establishment at nearby Boscombe Down in 1939. Continuing military employment in the area and the onset of commuting via the A303 have consolidated Amesbury's growth.

Above and right: Woodhenge. First identified following an aerial archaeological survey in 1925, this Neolithic monument 2 miles north-east of Stonehenge consisted of 168 post holes, most of which contained wooden posts which stood up to 7.5m above ground. Today concrete pillars mark the site of each post hole.

Stonehenge, one of the most famous sights in England. The complex was developed from perhaps as early as 3100BC until about 1600BC – a period of 1500 years – probably as a centre of ancestor worship.

Heale House and gardens. The house was originally built in the seventeenth century and was much smaller; it was considerably enlarged by the architect Detmar Blow after 1894, but in a way that makes it difficult to distinguish new from old.

Ludgershall Castle. A twelfth-century fortified royal residence, it was turned into a hunting lodge by Henry III but had fallen into disuse by the fifteenth century.

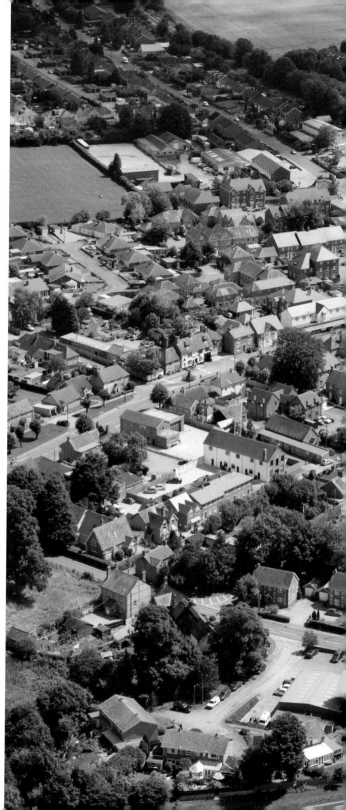

Ludgershall. From a small village of 535 in 1831, Ludgershall today has nearly 4000 residents and is officially a town. The parish church of St James can be seen in the centre of the picture to the left.

Above: Army training ground on the edge of Salisbury Plain near Ludgershall.

Opposite: Army trucks at military quarters in Tidworth, home to the 1st Mechanised Brigade.

The barracks at Tidworth are named after British Army battles in India and Afghanistan (including Assaye, Aliwal, Bhurtpore, Candahar, Lucknow and Delhi).

Previous page, above and opposite: Old Sarum. Lying at the top of a hill just over a mile to the north of modern Salisbury, its predecessor was enclosed within the earthworks of an Iron Age hill-fort. It consisted of a cathedral (whose outline can be seen clearly opposite), a castle on the central mound (above) and houses of the town's population (although most of these probably grew up outside of the earthworks). In the twelfth century the clergy and the garrison of the castle fell out increasingly and, with growing shortages of water, the clergy decided to move out and found New Sarum – Salisbury – in the valley below.

Fairground on the edge of Salisbury.

Salisbury United Reformed Church, Fisherton Street, built in 1879 (centre), and St Thomas of Canterbury church (top left) of the fifteenth century in St Thomas Square.

Above: Salisbury railway station, the crossing point of the Wessex Main Line and the West of England Main Line. The station was built originally by the London and South Western Railway.

Right: Salisbury and South Wiltshire Museum, at the top of the picture, is housed in the King's House, Cathedral Close, where James I was entertained in 1610 and 1613. The River Avon flows at the bottom of the picture.

41

Salisbury Cathedral.

Left: The magnificent West Front, over 33 metres high and wide, containing over 130 niches, 73 of which contain a statue.

Above: The spire at 404 feet (123m) is the tallest in the UK and - dating from 1320 – is the tallest surviving pre-1400 spire in the world.

Salisbury Cathedral. The Cloisters are the largest in Britain. To their right stands the octagonal Chapter House, completed like the Cloisters around 1280.

Salisbury Cathedral School was founded in 1091 by Saint Osmund at Old Sarum. It was moved 150 years later to the newly-built Salisbury Cathedral. In 1947 it was relocated to the former Bishop's Palace in the grounds of the cathedral.

Above: Market Place, Salisbury. Markets are held on Tuesdays and Saturdays.

Left: Salisbury. "New Sarum" received its first charter in 1227 and although in the past it had a flourishing cloth trade, today it is principally a tourist and market centre.

Godolphin School, Salisbury. Founded in 1726 for the education of eight orphaned gentlewomen, the independent boarding school now has a roll of some 420 girls. The writers Dorothy L. Sayers, Minette Walters and Jilly Cooper are amongst famous past pupils.

Wilton House. The first Earl of Pembroke was granted the estate of the Benedictine nunnery here in 1544. His house forms the core of the present mansion, one of the most famous in Britain, and which dominates the small town of Wilton, once the county town of Wiltshire.

Above: Silver Street, Wilton.

Left: Wilton has a colourful and important history dating back to the Anglo-Saxons although it has been eclipsed by neighbouring Salisbury. From the mid seventeenth century Wilton underwent a process of rebuilding which meant that nearly all traces of its medieval buildings have been removed from view. For centuries the town has been famous as a centre of carpet manufacture.

Above: The church of St Mary and St Nicholas, Wilton. In the Romanesque style by architect T.H. Wyatt, the church was built between 1841 and 1844 and includes a campanile 105 feet (32m) high.

Left: Wilton House, showing the classical South Front on the right, designed by Isaac de Caus in the 1630s, with the advice of the great English architect Inigo Jones. This wing became one of the most influential buildings in the country and was copied (more or less) by numerous other country houses in the following century.

Overleaf: The setting of Wilton House on the edge of the town.

The Palladian Bridge in the gardens at Wilton. It was designed by the ninth Earl of Pembroke in 1737 and executed by the builder-architect Roger Morris. It has been much imitated and versions exist, for example, at Stowe in Buckinghamshire and Prior Park on the outskirts of Bath.

Salisbury Racecourse. A flat racing venue about 4 miles west of Salisbury and 2 miles east of Wilton, it hosts around sixteen meetings between May and October. The Sovereign Stakes, run in August, is Salisbury's most valuable event and highest class race of the season.

Above: The church of St Mary and St Lawrence, Stratford Tony. This church is no longer used and is in the care of a preservation trust.

Opposite: Harvesting near East Martin.

Above and opposite: New Wardour Castle, near Tisbury. The Old Castle having been abandoned after the Civil War, the owners of the estate, the Arundell family, had to wait until the seventh and eighth Lords Arundell married heiresses in the eighteenth century before they could afford to build a new mansion. New Wardour Castle was designed in 1768 by James Paine and is the biggest Georgian house in Wiltshire. For many years in the twentieth century it was a school, but it is now divided into flats.

Old Wardour Castle. The fortified mansion was built in 1392 in the unusual form of a hexagon, for John, Lord Lovell. The estate was bought by Sir Thomas Arundell in 1547 and the house was modernized for his son in 1578 by the great Elizabethan architect Robert Smythson (who also built Longleat). The house was besieged during the Civil War in 1643-4, and was so severely damaged that it was abandoned.

Pythouse (or Pyt House), Newtown, rebuilt in 1805 to the design of John Benett, its owner.

Strip lynchets, Aucombe Bottom, near Mere, which suggest the presence of an active farming community in this part of south-west Wiltshire in pre-historic times.

Mere lies in the extreme south-west of the county, close to the border with Somerset and Dorset. It has long had a prominent role as a staging post between London and Exeter, from the days of the stagecoach to today's traveller on the nearby A303. In the 1700s, it was a centre of linen weaving and in the 1800s of silk manufacture.

Above: Hazard's Hill, Mere.

Right: Castle Hill, Mere, dominates the town. Richard, Earl of Cornwall, son of King John, built a castle on the mound in 1253 but over the centuries the stone from it has been taken to build houses in the settlement beneath so that little is now left other than the magnificent view.

Above: Stourhead House, built for the Hoare banking family between 1720 and 1724, with the wings added between 1792 and 1804. The central block was gutted by fire in 1902 but immediately reconstructed.

Opposite: Stourhead obelisk, built in 1746-7, rebuilt in 1839-40 and restored in 1853.

Stourhead gardens and lake. Stourhead is one of the most famous landscape gardens in the world, created in the eighteenth century with a circuit of classical and Gothic buildings around a highly picturesque lake formed by damming the River Stour. *Left:* the Palladian Bridge of 1762; *above:* the Temple of Flora built in 1744 to the designs of Henry Flitcroft.   Stourhead was given to the National Trust by Sir Henry Hoare in 1946.

Longleat House and gardens. Longleat is an enormous Elizabethen "prodigy" house, mainly designed by Robert Smythson, and completed about 1580, for Sir John Thynne. The Thynne family, subsequently Marquesses of Bath, live here still.

Longleat. The stables constructed by Sir Jeffry Wyatville, when he was also commissioned to undertake major alterations to the house, between 1801-11.

Longleat in its garden setting. Capability Brown and Humphry Repton created the lake to the left of the house. Between the house and the lake can be seen two of the new mazes commissioned by the present Marquess of Bath in the 1990s, the Lunar Maze and the Sun Maze.

Opposite: The hedge maze at Longleat was first laid out in 1975 by the designer Greg Bright. It is made up of more than 16,000 English yews and covers an area of around 0.6 hectares (1.48 acres). Within the maze there are six wooden bridges offering a view of the centre which is marked by an observation tower.

Above: Parascending off hill tops near Stanton St Bernard.

Above: Westbury is centred on its historic Market Place with the fourteenth-century All Saint's church behind it.

Left: Westbury railway station on the edge of Westbury town. As can be seen, it is an important junction where the South West Main Line intersects with the South Wales to South Coast Cross Country route. More than a third of a million passengers use the station each year.

Above: The Westbury White Horse. Although it is sometimes claimed that it was cut into the chalk in 878 to commemorate the victory of King Alfred over the Danes, there is no evidence for it before 1720. In the1950s it was set in concrete and painted white for ease of maintenance.

Left: Iron Age Bratton Camp lies immediately above the Westbury White Horse.

Above: St James church, Trowbridge, dates from the 1400s although it was heavily restored in the nineteenth century.

Right: Trowbridge is the county town of Wiltshire, and the third largest settlement in the county after Swindon and Salisbury. The conically-capped clock tower of Trowbridge Town Hall is prominent on the far left of the picture.

Holy Trinity church, on Stallard Street, Trowbridge, was built in 1838 to serve the growing outer parts of the town.

Fore Street, Trowbridge.

Above: Foot bridge over the Avon, leading to Holy Trinity church, Bradford on Avon.

Left: The medieval bridge over the River Avon, Bradford on Avon. The domed building on the left side of the bridge was originally a chapel but was later used as the town's lockup. The River Avon provided the motive power for a number of cloth mills that sprang up along its banks in the town, the remains of which are still much in evidence.

Above: Holy Trinity church, Bradford on Avon, has Norman origins although it has been altered on many occasions subsequently.

Right: Bradford on Avon. The town has many attractive houses, especially of the early eighteenth century which reflect the wealth of its cloth industry and the architectural influence of nearby Bristol and Bath.

The Town Hall in Bradford on Avon was built in 1855 to designs by Thomas Fuller of Bath, but considered by many to be too large for a town of this size. It has been converted subsequently to be the Roman Catholic church.

Tithe barn, Barton Farm Country Park, Bradford on Avon, with the River Avon on one side and the Kennet and Avon Canal on the other. The fourteenth-century barn is huge, at 180 feet long and 30 feet wide.

Bradford Lock on the Kennet and Avon Canal, crossed by the B3109. The Kennet and Avon Canal allows navigation between the Floating Harbour at Bristol and the River Thames at Reading.

United Reformed Church, Holt, in the centre-west of the county.

Above: The parish church of St Michael and All Angels, Melksham, a big Perpendicular church, although the tower at the west end dates only from 1845.

Right: With 20,000 inhabitants Melksham is the fifth biggest town in Wiltshire. It has a significant industrial base, including the Cooper Tire and Rubber Company which produces Cooper Avon and Avon Tyres.

Opposite: Caen Hill Locks, on the Kennet and Avon Canal between Rowde and Devizes. The 16 locks here are part of a larger group of 29 which allows the canal to rise 237 feet in 2 miles.

Above: Bath Road (A361) and the Kennet and Avon Canal at Devizes.

Overleaf: Devizes Castle. Although there has been a castle on the site since 1080, the present building is a Victorian confection, built for the Leach family who were local tradesmen.

The Town Hall, Devizes, designed by Thomas Baldwin of Bath from 1806-8, faces down St John's Street.

Devizes, showing the Market Cross, built in 1814 to designs by Benjamin Wyatt and L.J. Abington, to replace an earlier cross standing further to the south.

Opposite: The Devizes White Horse, cut onto a slope of Roundway Hill, was created in 1999 to replace an earlier one of 1845. It is the only one in Wiltshire to face to the right.

Above: King's Play Hill, is a 29.5 hectare Site of Special Scientific Interest, within the North Wessex Downs Area of Outstanding Natural Beauty.

The adventure playground at Bowood was first opened in 1978. The full-size pirate galleon called *The Centaur* was designed and constructed by Cornish boat builder Alistair Guy using timbers from the estate. The adventure playground is one of the most exciting and famous in the South West.

Bowood House and gardens. The seat of the Marquess of Lansdowne, the house seems very substantial, but in fact the major part of it – the "Big House", which stood between the surviving house and the lake – was demolished after the Second World War.

Bowood. The courtyards were closed on their south sides (top of the picture) by two wings added by Robert Adam. The Italianate tower is by Sir Charles Barry.

Lackham House, now Wiltshire College Lackham, opened in 1946 as an agricultural college, and also hosts a Museum of Agriculture and Rural Life.

Above: Lacock Abbey. After the Dissolution the abbey was bought by Sir William Sharington who converted it into a house. Later it was inherited by the Talbot family. Perhaps Lacock's most famous owner was William Fox Talbot who invented the process on which modern photography is based. The abbey and almost all of the village were given to the National Trust in 1944.

Left: Lacock village, with the church of St Cyriac in the top left corner. Because of its unspoiled appearance the village is much in demand as a film and television set.

Above and right: Corsham Court. In 1745 the Methuen family bought the house and in 1761-64 commissioned Capability Brown to re-design it and landscape the park, one of the examples of Brown as architect as well as landscape gardener. The picture opposite makes clear the close relationship between the house and the town of Corsham.

The High Street in the historic market town of Corsham. Although the town has traditionally been an agricultural, wool industry and quarrying centre, since the First World War it has been an important focus for military activity and today the Ministry of Defence employs some 2000 people in the area.

Castle Combe motor racing circuit. The circuit is based on the perimeter track of a Second World War airfield which was decommissioned in 1948. The race track opened in 1950. Although it continues to be a successful motor sport venue, the Formula 3 championship which used to be held here was forced from the circuit after a noise nuisance order was placed on it by the Local Authority.

Castle Combe and the church of St Andrew. The fourteenth-century Market Cross is under the pyramid roof in the centre of the village where the three main streets converge.

One of Biddestone's most significant features is the large village green, complete with duck pond, at the heart of the village.

Above: Malmesbury. The Market Cross at the top of the picture was built at the end of the fifteenth century and was, according to the antiquary John Leland "a place for poore folks to stande dry when rayne cummeth." It remains one of the finest in the country.

Left: Malmesbury is dominated by the remains of its great abbey. At one time the abbey had a spire taller than that of Salisbury Cathedral, but it collapsed before the Reformation. What is left is today the parish church.

Charlton Park. The ancestral home of the Earl of Suffolk and Berkshire, it was completed by 1607. The exterior is thoroughly Tudor/Jacobean, although the interior is largely Georgian and later.

Windmill Hill Business Park, Swindon. The park currently contains 670,000 sq feet of office space and when complete this will be nearer 1 million sq feet.

Above: The church of St John the Baptist and St Helen in Wroughton, with Wroughton House behind it.

Left: Wroughton lies some 4 miles south-east of Swindon but is part of the Borough of Swindon. The presence of RAF Wroughton, just south of the village, which was operational from the 1930s until the 1970s, had a significant impact on the settlement's growth.

Following the closure of RAF Wroughton, the site was transferred to the Science Museum to be used as a storage site. Now known as the Science Museum Swindon, around 20,000 objects are kept in six of the hangars, ranging from the first hovercraft to de-activated nuclear missiles.

Barbury Castle Iron Age hill-fort, on the ancient Ridgeway route, is now managed as a country park by Swindon Borough Council.

Marlborough College, Marlborough, is one of the foremost public schools in England. The sixth Duke of Somerset built a new house near the Norman castle mound, which was completed by 1723. This became the core of the College, which commenced in 1843 with 200 boys.

Above: Marlborough Town Hall (centre) was designed by C.E. Ponting in the style of the late seventeenth century.

Left: The High Street, Marlborough. Following a devastating fire in 1653 most of the town was rebuilt so there are few structures earlier than the late 1600s.

Hills at Preshute Downs and Marlborough Downs, part of the North Wessex Downs Area of Outstanding Natural Beauty.

Above and opposite: Avebury is one of the most important Neolithic monuments in Europe, consisting of a large henge, stone avenues and stone circles. Archaeologist Alexander Keiller re-erected many of the stones in the 1930s; a further 15 stones have been located lying buried on the site.

Overleaf: Silbury Hill, is part of the complex of Neolithic monuments near Avebury. It is the tallest prehistoric man-made "hill" in Europe, but its purpose has been subject to wide disagreement.

Opposite: The West Kennet Long Barrow, a Neolithic tomb near Silbury Hill.

Above: Littlecote House, on the banks of the River Kennet, is an Elizabthen mansion completed in 1592. Today it is a Warner Hotel and Resort.

New meets old in Wiltshire. An example of how the county supports a modern and vibrant industry (in this case tourism) in the midst of its historic landscape – the swimming pool at Center Parcs Longleat Forest, near Warminster.